# Sociology in Pictures
## Theories and Concepts

# Michael Haralambos
## with Wendy Hope     Illustrated by Matt Timson

## Contents

**Published by Collins Educational**

An imprint of HarperCollins Publishers, 77-85 Fulham Palace Road, Hammersmith, London W6 8JB

© Michael Haralambos, 2013

10 9 8 7 6 5 4 3 2 1

ISBN 978-0-00-754266-6

Michael Haralambos asserts his moral rights to be identified as the author of this work.

British Library Cataloguing in Publication Data.
A catalogue record for this publication is available from the British Library.

**Typography and design** by John A Collins

**Printed and bound** in the UK by www.waringcollins.com

**Thanks** To Peter Langley who, with Michael Haralambos, developed the idea of sociology in pictures. And thanks to Alexandra Riley and Katie Nelson at Collins Educational for their support.

**Dedication** To Charlie, Sammy, Max, Miles, Isab..ttie and Woody

North West Kent College

070309

# CULTURE

Culture is the learned, shared behaviour of members of society. It includes norms – accepted and expected ways of behaving; values – beliefs about what is worth having and worth striving for; and roles – the parts people play in society.

## NORMS OF TALKING

Norms define the appropriate distance between people when they talk. These norms are different between North and South America (Hall, 1973).

## NORMS OF DRESS

In the 19th century, a Western missionary imported bras for the women he was trying to convert. The results were not what he expected.

## VALUES AND BRAVERY

The traditional culture of the Plains tribes of the USA placed a high value on bravery. One of the bravest acts was counting coup – striking an enemy with a wooden coup stick.

## MARITAL ROLES

Polygyny – one man married to two or more women – is found in many traditional small-scale societies, particularly in Africa (Brazier, 1995).

# SOCIAL CONTROL

Social control refers to mechanisms which enforce society's norms and rules. Some types of social control can be seen in a positive light — it is difficult to see how society could operate without them. Others can be seen in a negative light — as keeping people in their place and maintaining the position of the rich and powerful. Here are some examples of the many forms of social control.

## FORMAL CONTROL

Formal methods of social control are specifically set up for that purpose — for example, the world's first police force established in London in 1829.

## INFORMAL CONTROL

Though not specifically designed for the purpose, informal methods can result in social control. For example, well-lit streets encourage a sense of community, which can lead to informal controls such as gossip and public surveillance, which can deter crime.

## RELIGION

Religion can provide social control in various ways. Here, archbishops are performing a coronation and giving their blessing to the rule of an evil tyrant.

## SANCTIONS

Sanctions — rewards and punishments — are obvious forms of social control. In traditional Cheyenne society, parents punished babies for crying by hanging their cradleboards from trees and leaving them until they stopped.

# MARXISM

Karl Marx (1818-1883), the founder of Marxism, believed that the economic system – the forces of production – shaped the rest of society. If everybody owns the forces of production, the result is an equal society. But if they are owned by a minority, society is made up of two main social classes – a rich and powerful ruling class and a relatively poor and powerless subject class. Marx saw the ruling class as exploiting and oppressing the subject class.

## FEUDALISM

In medieval Europe, the land – the main force of production – was owned by the lords (the ruling class) and farmed by serfs (the subject class). The serfs paid taxes to the lords in cash and produce. This system is called feudalism.

## CAPITALISM

In industrial society, the forces of production – the factories and raw materials – are owned by the capitalist ruling class. The workers – the subject class – produce the goods but their wages are only a small part of the value of those goods. Most of the value is taken away in the form of profits by the capitalists. Marx saw this as exploitation.

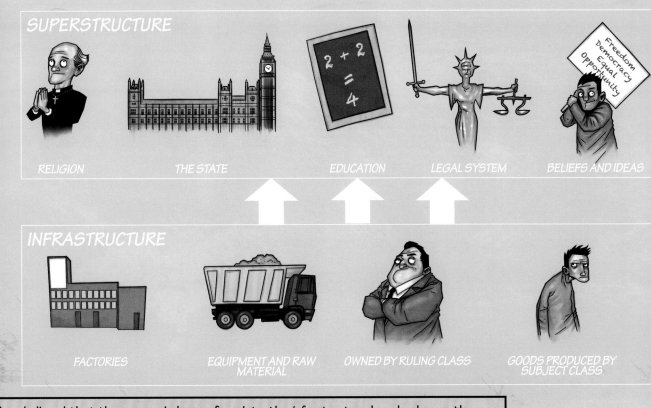

SUPERSTRUCTURE

RELIGION · THE STATE · EDUCATION · LEGAL SYSTEM · BELIEFS AND IDEAS

INFRASTRUCTURE

FACTORIES · EQUIPMENT AND RAW MATERIAL · OWNED BY RULING CLASS · GOODS PRODUCED BY SUBJECT CLASS

Marx believed that the economic base of society, the *infrastructure*, largely shapes the rest of society, the *superstructure*. This means that the economic relationships between the ruling and subject class will be reflected in the superstructure. For example, the state will support the ruling class and pass laws to reinforce their economic power and control.

## RULING CLASS IDEOLOGY

WE OWN THE FACTORIES SO WE HAVE A RIGHT TO TAKE PROFITS.

THIS IS FALSE BECAUSE WORKERS PRODUCE PROFITS, NOT OWNERS.

YOU LIVE IN A FREE SOCIETY. YOU HAVE THE FREEDOM TO CHOOSE YOUR JOB AND LEAVE IT WHEN YOU WANT.

THIS IS FALSE BECAUSE PEOPLE MUST WORK TO SURVIVE. ONLY A LIMITED CHOICE OF JOBS.

WE LIVE IN A DEMOCRATIC SOCIETY SON. YOU VOTE FOR THOSE WHO GOVERN YOU. THE CHOICE IS YOURS.

THIS IS FALSE BECAUSE NO REAL CHOICE. ALL PARTIES SUPPORT THE CAPITALIST SYSTEM.

I WANT YOUR VOTE. AS YOUR MEMBER OF PARLIAMENT, I WILL REPRESENT YOU.

THIS IS FALSE BECAUSE MPS WILL REPRESENT THE RULING CLASS.

According to Marx, the ideas and beliefs in society reinforce and justify ruling class power and blind the subject class to their exploitation. Marx called these ideas and beliefs *ruling class ideology*. He saw ideology as producing a *false consciousness* - a distorted and untrue view of the way things are.

Members of Parliament representing the ruling class.

RELIGION

In Marx's words, 'Religion is the opium of the people'. Opium is an hallucinatory drug which creates illusions and eases pain. Marx believed that religion disguises the exploitation of class society and soothes the pain exploitation produces.

# THE REVOLUTION

Marx believed that the workers would eventually see society as it really was. They would overthrow capitalism and replace it with communism – an equal society in which the forces of production were owned by all the people.

# THE STATE 'WITHERS AWAY'

Marx believed that when communism replaced capitalism there would be no need for the state. The state would 'wither away' and people would govern themselves.

# ALIENATION

Marx saw work as the most important human activity. He argued that in capitalist society people are alienated or cut off from their work. As a result, they are alienated from themselves, from others and from the things they produce. Alienation will only end when the forces of production are communally owned.

## KARL MARX

THE ALIENATED WORKER DOES NOT FULFIL HIMSELF, HAS A FEELING OF MISERY, IS MENTALLY DEBASED.

Work is the way for people to express their true humanity, their essential selves. Alienated from work, they cannot do this. They are dehumanised.

## FORCED LABOUR

Alienation will only end in a society where people are free to work both for themselves and everybody else. In capitalism, work is 'forced labour, performed in the service, under the coercion and the yoke of another'.

## COMMODITIES

I HAVE TO WORK TO SURVIVE.

MAKING THIS IS A MEANS TO AN END.

I'M ONLY HERE FOR THE MONEY.

Workers are alienated from the product of their labour. It does not belong to them. It is simply a commodity to be sold and bought.

## WORKERS

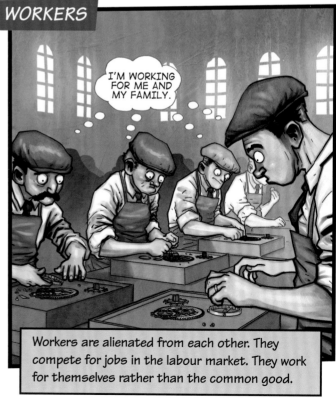

I'M WORKING FOR ME AND MY FAMILY.

Workers are alienated from each other. They compete for jobs in the labour market. They work for themselves rather than the common good.

# EMILE DURKHEIM

The French sociologist Emile Durkheim (1858-1917), often seen as the founder of modern sociology, argued that one of the main functions of society's parts was to provide 'the essential similarities which collective life demands'. These similarities provide the basis for cooperation, order, 'collective conscience' (shared moral beliefs) and 'social solidarity' (social unity).

## ESSENTIAL SIMILARITIES

## WORKING TOGETHER

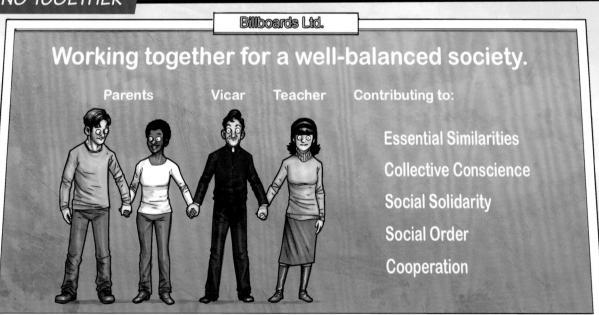

Durkheim compared society with an organism in which the various parts, such as the heart and lungs, work together for the benefit of the organism as a whole. Similarly, in a well-balanced society, the various parts, for example families, schools and religion, combine to benefit society as a whole.

# ANOMIE

Durkheim used the term *anomie* to describe his view of industrial society at the close of the 19th century. Anomie means normlessness. Without norms people develop limitless desires, insatiable appetites and feelings of dissatisfaction. Anomie occurs at times of rapid social change when old norms break down and new ones have yet to replace them.

## NORMS AND NO NORMS

Norms place limits on people's desires and expectations. Anomie leads to unlimited desires which can never be satisfied.

## DURKHEIM

REALITY SEEMS VALUELESS BY COMPARISON WITH THE DREAMS OF FEVERED IMAGINATIONS.

## DISSATISFACTION

MONEY, MONEY, MONEY.

GOLD TAPS FOR THE BATH, A PLATINUM TIARA FOR MY PARTNER, BUT I'M STILL MISERABLE.

The more she gets, the more she wants.

## ANOMIC SUICIDE

A Baltimore banker who has lost all his money in a recession blows himself up. Based on a French painting from 1900.

Anomie increases in times of both boom and bust. Durkheim found that suicide rates rose during periods of rapid economic change.

# FUNCTIONALISM

Functionalism was the dominant theory in sociology in the 1940s and 50s. Following Durkheim, it saw society as a system, as a set of parts which made up a whole. One of the main aims of functionalism is to examine the function of each part – the contribution it makes to the well-being of society as a whole. Here are some examples.

A function of the family – teaches children the norms and values of society.

A function of religion – reinforces society's norms and values.

A function of schools – teaches young people to achieve as individuals, a skill they will need as adults.

A function of social inequality – society's most important jobs are highly rewarded so people will compete for them and the most talented will win through. This will benefit society as a whole.

# FUNCTIONS OF RELIGION

Here are two classic interpretations of the functions of religion, the first by the French sociologist, Emile Durkheim, the second by the Polish anthropologist, Bronislaw Malinowski.

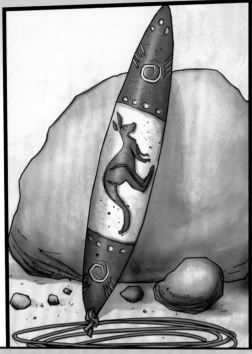

An Australian Aboriginal bullroarer, a sacred object carved with a religious symbol or 'totem'.

The clan was the main social group in Aboriginal society. Each clan had a totem, in this case a kangaroo. In Durkheim's words, the totem 'is at once the symbol of god and of the society'. In worshipping the totem the unity of the clan is strengthened by supernatural power.

The Trobriand Islanders hold a religious ceremony before fishing in the sometimes rough and dangerous waters beyond the barrier reef, but not before fishing in the calm and safe waters of the lagoon. Malinowski argues that religion functions to reduce anxiety by giving a feeling of security and sense of control.

# MAX WEBER

Max Weber ( 1864-1920) is one of the founding fathers of sociology. His social action theory states that human action is directed by meanings. The job of the sociologist is to interpret these meanings. Weber's approach can be seen from his study, *The Protestant Ethic and the Spirit of Capitalism* in which he argued that meanings derived from 'ascetic Protestantism' produced the 'spirit of capitalism' which led to Western industrial capitalism. (Ascetic means abstaining from pleasure, severe self-discipline.)

THE GODLY AND HARD-WORKING MAN SHALL HAVE PROSPERITY.

HE THAT FOLLOWS PLEASURES SHALL HAVE MUCH SORROW.

John Browne, a 16th century Protestant.

KEEP OUT. YOU COME NOT HERE.

O SIR, I BRING YOU GOOD CHEER,

A Puritan drives Father Christmas out of town – based on a cartoon from 1653. Christmas fun and games and even mince pies were banned in mid-17th century England.

RELIGION MUST NECESSARILY PRODUCE HARD WORK AND DISCOURAGE THE WASTING OF MONEY.

John Wesley (1703-1791) the founder of Methodism.

REMEMBER THAT TIME IS MONEY. ALWAYS BE EMPLOYED IN SOMETHING USEFUL.

Benjamin Franklin (1706-1790) who Weber saw as embodying the spirit of capitalism.

According to Weber, the Protestant ethic saw work as a religious calling, success in business as indicating that a person had not lost favour in God's eyes, and profits as a source for further investment in business rather than a means of funding luxuries and frivolous entertainment.

# RATIONAL ACTION

Weber argued that action in modern industrial society is based on reason rather than tradition and emotion. He called this type of action *instrumental rational action*. It is a way of achieving a goal based on precise calculation and measurement. It involves an assessment of the various ways of achieving that goal. In a rational world science replaces religion, reason replaces faith. Weber saw the result as 'disenchantment of the world' – a cold, calculating and soulless outlook on society.

## WEATHER

The Hopi of Arizona performing a rain dance to influence the supernatural powers to bring rain.

Forecasting the weather in terms of the science of meteorology.

## MEDICINE

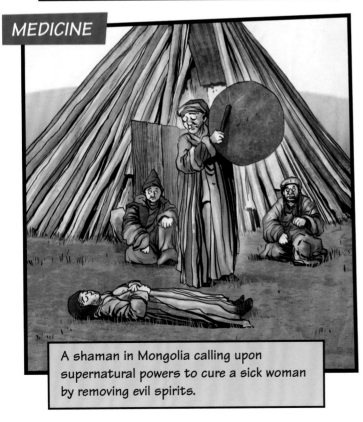

A shaman in Mongolia calling upon supernatural powers to cure a sick woman by removing evil spirits.

Medical science has largely replaced ideas about supernatural explanations and cures for illness.

## BUREAUCRACY

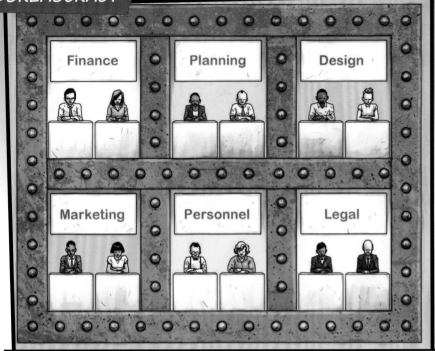

## WEBER

RATIONAL CALCULATION REDUCES EVERY WORKER TO A COG IN THE BUREAUCRATIC MACHINE.

For Weber, instrumental rational action is seen most clearly in bureaucracies. They are based on specific rules and regulations, specialist skills, precise calculation and well-defined goals. They are capable of 'attaining the highest degree of efficiency'. But, bureaucracy can imprison workers in an 'iron cage', produce 'specialists without spirit' and work against spontaneity,

## CONSUMERISM

Weber argued that rational thinking led to the pursuit of wealth and material goods being 'stripped of its religious and ethical meaning'. He believed that 'material goods have gained an increasing and finally an inexorable (unstoppable) power over the lives of people as at no previous period in history'.

# STRATIFICATION

Social stratification refers to inequalities between groups in society. Max Weber identifies three main forms — stratification based on, 1) economic, 2) status and 3) power inequalities.

## CLASS

According to Weber, a class consists of people who have a similar economic or *market situation* – similar 'goods and opportunities for income'. Weber identified four classes: 1) an upper class whose income derives from property – ownership of companies, land, mines; 2) a class of professionals (doctors, lawyers) and white-collar workers; 3) a class of small business owners; 4) a class of manual workers.

## LIFE CHANCES

Weber states that people in the same class usually have similar *life chances* – living standards, housing, health and life expectancy.

## STATUS

Status refers to the unequal distribution of 'social honour' and prestige. Often high class and high status go together, but not always – for example, the penniless aristocrat belonging to a high status group.

Weber sees status groups as having *social closure*. People without the appropriate lifestyle, taste and manners would tend to find membership of a status group closed to them.

Weber sees status groups reaching their most developed form in the Hindu caste system in India. The lowest level, the Dalits, were seen as unclean and impure by other status groups. The picture shows a man dropping wages wrapped in a leaf to Dalit workers to avoid the pollution which contact is seen to produce.

## PARTIES

Weber calls the third type of stratification *parties*. Parties are concerned with representing the interests of their members. They often represent class and/or status groups but not always. In Weber's words, 'In most cases they are partly class parties and partly status parties, but sometimes they are neither'.

An early Labour Party poster. Founded in 1900, the Labour Party aimed to represent the working class. It now claims to represent the nation as a whole.

Parties include professional bodies like the British Medical Association, trade unions, and campaign groups such as Greenpeace and Friends of the Earth.

# THE CHICAGO SCHOOL

In the first half of the 20th century, sociologists at the University of Chicago developed an approach to the study of cities, known as urban ecology. The Chicago School argued that people's behaviour is shaped by their environment. They saw the growth of cities leading to the formation of different neighbourhoods, each of which produced different patterns of behaviour.

## THE CHICAGO SCHOOL

GO GET THE SEAT OF YOUR PANTS DIRTY IN REAL RESEARCH.

The 'Chicago School' was chaired by Robert Park, who sent his students into the 'luxury hotels' and the 'flophouses' to gather data.

## CRIME RATES

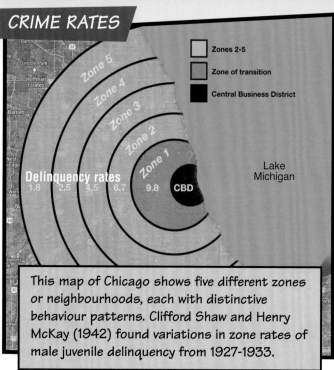

This map of Chicago shows five different zones or neighbourhoods, each with distinctive behaviour patterns. Clifford Shaw and Henry McKay (1942) found variations in zone rates of male juvenile delinquency from 1927-1933.

## SOCIAL DISORGANISATION

WE'VE COME A LONG WAY FROM ALABAMA.

I'VE GOT A NEW JOB SO WE'RE MOVING TO A BETTER NEIGHBOURHOOD.

Zone 1 has the highest rate of delinquency. This *zone of transition* is a low-income, inner-city area with a high population turnover, as migrants move in and others move out. Shaw and McKay argue that this produces instability which results in *social disorganisation*. This in turn leads to weak social controls which allow high rates of crime to develop.

## CULTURAL HETEROGENEITY

Black and white rural migrants from the southern states and migrants from Ireland, Italy, Greece and Poland moved into Chicago's zone of transition bringing with them a variety of cultures. This *cultural heterogeneity* (diversity) contributed to social disorganisation by preventing the formation of a uniform culture and so weakening social controls such as public disapproval and surveillance.

## NEIGHBOURHOOD EFFECTS

The concentric zone pattern does not fit British or even some American cities. Here are some alternative views of delinquency and the urban environment.

A study of Croydon suggests that delinquency rates reflected local authority housing policies. High rates were found on estates where the council had housed large numbers of so-called 'problem families', whose members often had a history of delinquency (Morris, 1957).

A study of low-income black neighbourhoods in Chicago found high levels of delinquency despite stable populations and a single culture. The researchers argue that this was due to 'low levels of informal social control' with parents feeling they had 'little control over their children' (Wilson, 1996).

# SYMBOLIC INTERACTIONISM

The American philosopher George Herbert Mead (1863-1931) is one of the founders of symbolic interactionism. According to Mead, human beings interact in terms of meanings which make sense of actions, objects and events. Meanings provide a definition of the situation which directs how people act.

## MEANINGS

The way people interpret and define the bandaged figure will shape their actions towards him or her.

## ROLE-TAKING

People give meaning to the actions of others by role-taking – putting themselves in the place of others and interpreting others' responses.

## SELF

When role-taking, individuals are able to look back at themselves. In this way, they develop a concept of self. This happens when a child plays a make-believe role.

## SELF AND OTHERS

With an awareness of self, a person can set their own goals and direct their own actions. And by role-taking, they are aware of what others expect from them. They are now both an individual and a member of society.

# INTERACTION PROCESSES

## LOOKING-GLASS SELF

A person's picture of self comes, in part, from their perception of how others see them. This is known as their looking-glass self.

## SELF-FULFILLING PROPHECY

A person's looking-glass self can produce a self-fulfilling prophecy – a prediction that comes to pass. They tend to act in terms of the way they believe others see them.

## LABELLING THEORY

A label is a definition of a person applied by others. The American sociologist, Howard Becker, states that 'deviant behaviour is behaviour that people so label'. Becker argues that the police have a picture of the typical delinquent which they are likely to apply to people who fit this picture. A label can become a master status – a dominant status which overrides all other statuses.

# ACTING THE PART

In *The Presentation of Self in Everyday Life*, Erving Goffman (1959) compares social interaction with acting in a play. We present ourselves to an audience, give a performance, attempt to create an impression, adopt an appropriate manner, make use of suitable props and, like actors, play particular parts in different situations.

## A PERFORMANCE

Playing the part of an agreeable shop assistant.

## USING PROPS

A judge, barrister and solicitor set a tone with various props — wigs, costumes, a gavel and documents tied with ribbons.

## IMPRESSION MANAGEMENT

The setting, the costume and the name all create an impression.

## A FAILED PERFORMANCE

As far as the patient is concerned, this is a failed performance.

# ETHNOMETHODOLOGY

Ethnomethodology means the study of the methods used by people. This approach was founded by the American sociologist Harold Garfinkel (1967). He argues that members of society assume that the social world is ordered and makes sense. However, this order and sense may not actually exist. Instead it may be constructed to make the social world appear knowable, reasonable and understandable.

## A COUNSELLING EXPERIMENT

Students asked a counsellor in a university psychiatry department questions about a personal problem. The counsellor – an actor – gave random yes or no answers. The students made sense of the answers where no sense existed.

## INDEXICALITY

Students made sense of the answers by placing them in a particular context – a psychiatry department. This method is called *indexicality*.

## A BREACHING EXPERIMENT

Students were asked to act as boarders in their own home. This is a 'breaching experiment', it disrupts normal routines. It shows how people attempt to construct order and manufacture sense when expected patterns of behaviour are breached.

## DOCUMENTARY METHOD

Making sense involves assuming an underlying pattern (her daughter is ill) and interpreting the situation in terms of this pattern. This is called the *documentary method*.

# PHENOMENOLOGY

Phenomenology is an approach which states that things and events have no meaning in themselves. They only mean what people take them to mean. This is the view of J. Maxwell Atkinson in *Discovering Suicide* (1978). He argues that suicide is simply a meaning given to an event. There is no such thing as a 'real' or 'objective' suicide death waiting to be discovered. The job of the sociologist is therefore to discover now 'deaths get categorised as suicide'.

Atkinson argues that coroners have a 'common sense theory of suicide' which includes a 'typical suicide biography' and 'typical suicide death'. The nearer a death fits this theory, the more likely it will be classified as suicide.

Atkinson argues that coroners make 'otherwise disordered and potentially senseless events, ordered and sensible'.

# FEMINISM

Feminists have brought women into the mainstream of sociology. They have catalogued the inequalities between women and men, provided explanations for them and suggested routes to equality. There are many feminist views. Here are some of them.

## LIBERAL FEMINISM

Liberal feminists demand equal rights for women. They believe this can be achieved by laws banning discrimination and providing equal opportunities. In the UK, the Equal Pay Act (1970) and the Sex Discrimination Act (1975) went some way towards meeting their demands.

## MARXIST FEMINISM

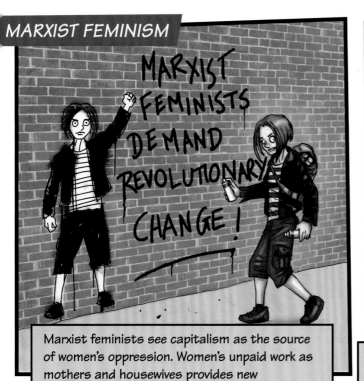

Marxist feminists see capitalism as the source of women's oppression. Women's unpaid work as mothers and housewives provides new generations of workers at no cost to capitalists.

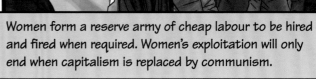

Women form a reserve army of cheap labour to be hired and fired when required. Women's exploitation will only end when capitalism is replaced by communism.

## RADICAL FEMINISM

Radical feminists see *patriarchy*, the systematic oppression of women by men, as the cause of women's exploitation. They see patriarchy as present in every area of life, across all cultures and throughout history. Here are two instances.

> WIVES, SUBMIT YOURSELVES TO YOUR HUSBANDS, AS IS FIT IN THE LORD.

Early Christian beliefs according to St Paul.

Based on a drawing by George Cruickshank, 1847. Some radical feminists argue that male dominance is ultimately maintained by force.

## BLACK FEMINISM

African-American sociologists argue that theories should take racial discrimination into account. According to Patricia Hill Collins (1990), 'stereotypical mammies, matriarchs, welfare recipients and hot mammas' are some of the images used to control black women. Will Michelle Obama help to change these views?

## POSTMODERN FEMINISM

Postmodern feminists argue that there is no universal essence of womanhood. Women differ widely in terms of class, culture, ethnicity, nationality, age, religion and sexual orientation. No single theory can explain this diversity.

# GENDER

Sociologists sometimes distinguish between sex – the biological differences between women and men, and gender – the cultural differences between women and men. This leads them to ask: Are the differences between female and male roles due to biology or to culture or to a combination of both?

## BIOLOGY

A survey of 224 societies by George Peter Murdock (1949) found that men with their 'superior physical strength' performed more 'strenuous tasks' while women with 'physiological burdens of pregnancy and nursing performed lighter tasks nearer the home'.

## CULTURE

In many traditional African societies women did most of the heavy work – farming, building huts and granaries and fetching water and wood. This suggests that gender roles are shaped by culture rather than biology.

## THREE GENDERS

Many Native American tribes identified a third gender – 'two-spirit' people who were doubly blessed with the spirit of a man and a woman. The picture shows We'wha, a Zuni two-spirit person (Williams, 1991).

## GENDER DIVERSITY

Some researchers argue that the female/male distinction does not reflect gender diversity – masculine women and feminine men, transsexuals, transvestites, bisexuals, gays, lesbians, heterosexuals.

# MICHEL FOUCAULT

The French historian and philosopher Michel Foucault (1926-1984) has had an important influence on sociology, particularly with his idea of *discourse*. A discourse is a way of knowing, thinking and understanding. Discourses form the basis for our actions. They provide our reality. Foucault saw his job as a historian to discover discourses and show how they arise and how they are replaced. This unit gives a flavour of his approach from his first major work, *History of Madness* (2009), which analyses three discourses of 'madness'.

## THE RENAISSANCE

During the Renaissance the 'mad' were seen to have special insight and knowledge. In their 'innocent idiocy' they have 'the wisdom of fools'. In art and literature the Ship of Fools is a recurring theme. It shows 'mad' people expelled from towns in 'ships of fools'.

## THE CLASSICAL AGE

In 17th century Europe the 'great confinement of the mad' took place. The new sin was idleness and sloth. The 'mad' must be punished and put to work. Their 'madness' was now seen as 'unreason' rather than the 'wisdom of fools'.

Jean-Baptiste Colbert, Louis X1V's Minister of Finance. In 1656 the king ordered the Hospital General to be built in Paris to confine the 'mad', the beggars, the poor, the unemployed and criminals.

## THE MODERN AGE

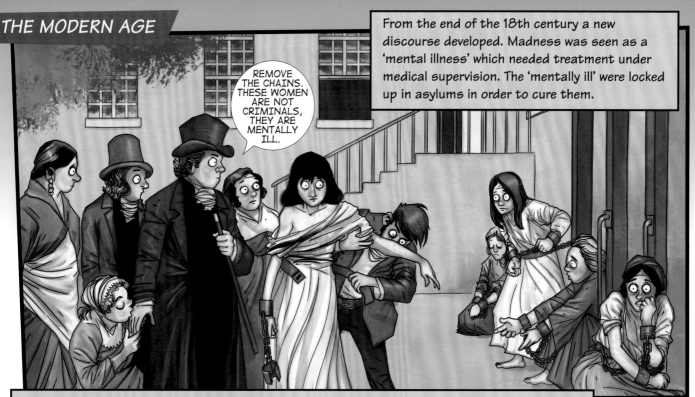

From the end of the 18th century a new discourse developed. Madness was seen as a 'mental illness' which needed treatment under medical supervision. The 'mentally ill' were locked up in asylums in order to cure them.

REMOVE THE CHAINS. THESE WOMEN ARE NOT CRIMINALS, THEY ARE MENTALLY ILL.

Doctor Philippe Pinel ordering the removal of chains from patients in the Paris Asylum for 'insane' women. Based on a 1795 painting by Robert Fleury. Sometimes described as the 'father of modern psychiatry', Pinel published a classification of 'mental illnesses'.

## ARCHAEOLOGY

DOING HISTORY MEANS DIGGING FOR DISCOURSES.

The Past →

Foucault called his historical method 'the archaeology of knowledge'. He argued that to understand behaviour historians must unearth the discourses which direct and control behaviour.

## POWER

POWER IS KNOWLEDGE AND KNOWLEDGE IS POWER.

Foucault saw history as a battle between groups to establish their discourses as the truth. Those who win have considerable power. For example, psychiatrists have the power to define normality and abnormality.

# PIERRE BOURDIEU

The French sociologist Pierre Bourdieu (1930-2002) argues that the higher a person's position in the class system, the more likely they are to have greater amounts of cultural, social, economic and symbolic capital. Cultural capital refers to manners, taste, knowledge and language skills, social capital to social contacts, economic capital to income and wealth, and symbolic capital to status and prestige.

## CAPITAL

A family with considerable capital: cultural – an appreciation of the arts, social – useful contacts, economic – a house worth £10 million, symbolic – an MBE.

## ROUTES TO THE TOP

Prime Minister David Cameron and Chancellor of the Exchequer George Osborne. Economic capital paid for their expensive public schools. They accumulated social capital at Oxford where important contacts were made. At the Bullingdon dining club their cultural capital stood them in good stead. And with over two-thirds of the Cabinet in 2010 from public schools, they found themselves in similar company (House of Commons Library, 2013).

Bourdieu's ideas have been influential in the study of education. Here they are used to explain class differences in educational attainment.

Bourdieu (1984) claims that educational success depends largely on the culture learned in the child's early years. Since education is based on the culture of the 'dominant classes', their children are usually the most successful – they have most cultural capital.

Research in London primary schools showed that middle-class mothers used their cultural and economic capital to good effect. They were more likely than working-class mothers to help their children with homework and to pay for extra tuition (Reay, 1998).

Middle-class mothers often make considerable use of their social and cultural capital when choosing schools for their children – talking to teachers and friends and assessing the available evidence (Ball, 2003).

Middle-class students from public schools are most likely to choose elite universities like Oxford and Cambridge. Their cultural and social capital gives them the 'confidence, certainty and sense of entitlement' to make this choice (Reay et al., 2005).

Bordieu concludes that the role of education is social reproduction – 'the reproduction of the established order', of the power and privilege of the 'dominant classes'.

# POSTMODERN SOCIETY

Some sociologists believe that during the second half of the 20th century we moved from *modern* to *postmodern society*. Here are some of the factors they see as characteristic of postmodern society.

## ELECTRONIC MEDIA

In postmodern society electronic media engulf us with a multitude of meanings, messages and images. Exposure to multiple realities can make life seem rootless, fragmented, empty and meaningless.

## LOSS OF FAITH

WIND POWER IS THE WAY FORWARD. IT IS CLEAN AND SAFE.

NUCLEAR IS CHEAPER AND MORE RELIABLE.

There has been a loss of faith in science , medicine and technology. Differing views on a range of issues have questioned the objectivity of so-called experts.

## ALTERNATIVES

NEW AGE

Exposure to differing lifestyles can weaken established beliefs. A range of alternatives such as New Age religions and complementary medicine are becoming increasingly popular.

## IDENTITIES

WE'RE GAY. I'M A DESIGNER AND PAINTER. WE'RE KEEN GARDENERS.

I'M A MUSICIAN. WE BOTH BELONG TO GREENPEACE.

There is increasing freedom to create and express your identity in postmodern society and to have several identities to put on and take off, depending on the situation.

## REALITY AND ILLUSION

New York, Paris and Luxor – themed hotels in Las Vegas. According to the French philosopher Jean Baudrillard (1994), postmodern society blurs the line between reality and illusion. We live in a world of 'hyperreality' where illusion becomes real, and simulations become authentic.

## BEALE STREET

Beale Street, Memphis, the 'home of the blues'. Fifty years after its heyday, it has been recreated for tourists. Blues has all but died out in black communities. Music resembling blues blares from bars. But it can be seen as hyperreality – it has little or no depth, it is a second-rate copy, it merely simulates.

# LATE MODERNITY

Some sociologists reject the idea of a postmodern society. They argue that society has entered a later stage of modernity rather than a brand new era. The British sociologist Anthony Giddens (1991, 2009) takes this view, arguing that we are now living in *late modernity*.

## THE JUGGERNAUT

Giddens sees late modernity as a 'world of rapid change'. It is like 'a juggernaut, a runaway engine of enormous power which we can drive to some extent but which also threatens to rush out of our control'. The ride can be exhilarating but never entirely secure as it is 'fraught with risk' and uncertainty.

## THE REFLEXIVE SELF

In the rapidly changing society of late modernity, identity ceases to be clearly defined. As a result, people become increasingly reflexive – the self becomes 'something to be reflected on, altered, even moulded'. For example, the body becomes 'a visible carrier of self-identity', as we transform our appearance with diet, exercise, tattoos, piercing, cosmetic surgery, hairstyles and clothes. And we become increasingly dependent on experts to help us do this.

## SOCIAL REFLEXIVITY

When custom and tradition no longer direct behaviour, people become socially reflexive. They reflect on society and their situation, they question their actions and decisions, they choose between a range of alternatives.

## CONFLUENT LOVE

Giddens argues that intimate relationships in late modern society are increasingly based on 'confluent love' – on a deep, emotional closeness in which partners reveal their needs and concerns to each other. Without confluent love, they are likely to end the relationship.

## RISK AND TRUST

We recognise the risks of living in late modernity – financial crises, climate change, nuclear catastrophes. Trust involves having confidence in the agencies who deal with such matters, in people we don't know or never meet. This type of trust is, in Giddens' words, 'the subject of reflection and revision'.

# THE SECOND MODERNITY

The German sociologist Ulrich Beck (1992, 2001) believes we have moved into a new phase of modernity. He calls this phase the *second modernity*. It is characterised by risk and individualisation.

## THE RISK SOCIETY

Processed foods are a major risk factor. They can lead to obesity and health problems.

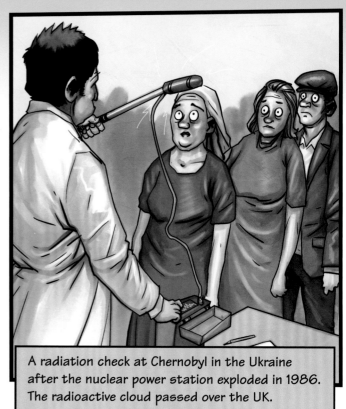

A radiation check at Chernobyl in the Ukraine after the nuclear power station exploded in 1986. The radioactive cloud passed over the UK.

Oil spill in the Gulf of Mexico, 2010. Pollution of land, sea and air is a global risk.

In the second modernity, the job market is increasingly unstable with job changes, short-term contracts and retraining more frequent. Relationships are more fragile with rising divorce and separation rates. Risk and uncertainty characterise life.

# INDIVIDUALISATION

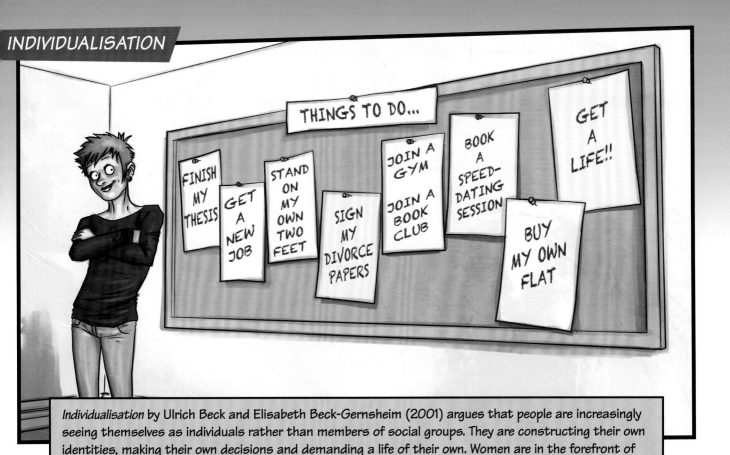

*Individualisation* by Ulrich Beck and Elisabeth Beck-Gernsheim (2001) argues that people are increasingly seeing themselves as individuals rather than members of social groups. They are constructing their own identities, making their own decisions and demanding a life of their own. Women are in the forefront of this process of individualisation.

## ALTRUISTIC INDIVIDUALISM

The second modernity is not a 'me-first society'. *Altruistic individualism* – concern for others while retaining individuality – is needed to live a life of your own.

## COOPERATIVE INDIVIDUALISM

People see relationships based on love as a refuge in 'our impersonal, uncertain society'. For love to succeed, it must be based on *cooperative individualism* – working together *and* having a life of your own. But this can lead to conflict and the break up of relationships.

# LIQUID MODERNITY

Zygmunt Bauman is Professor of Sociology at the Universities of Leeds and Warsaw. He calls the latest stage of modernity *liquid modernity*. It is fluid, flowing and flexible. 'Change is *the only* permanence and uncertainty *the only* certainty.'

## LIQUID SOCIETY

Bauman (2012) states, 'Living under liquid modern conditions can be compared to walking in a minefield: everyone knows that an explosion might happen at any moment.' Relationships are frail and fractious, jobs often temporary and insecure, nothing is certain.

## WORK

'Working life is saturated with insecurity' in liquid modernity. Short-term contracts, rolling contracts, redundancy and retraining are increasingly common.

## IDENTITY

In earlier stages of modernity, people's identity was largely fixed by their gender, occupation and class. Liquid modernity brings individualisation which gives people the freedom to create their own identities.

## LIQUID LOVE

Bauman (2003) sees the bonds between couples in liquid modernity as fragile. There is a conflict between the desire for individual freedom and the need for security. This means that the bonds have to be 'loosely tied so they can be untied with little delay' should relationships prove unsatisfactory. The result is 'semi-detached couples' in 'top pocket relationships' – people can pull their partner out of their pocket when required.

## SELF-BLAME

Individualisation is a mixed blessing. It gives freedom to create identities. But it can place blame for failure on individuals. Especially for the poor and powerless, the loss of a job or a partner can result in self-blame and 'broken, loveless and prospectless lives'.

## INDIVIDUALISATION

*The citizen*          *The individualist*

Individualisation is central to liquid modernity. People tend to see their lives as 'full of risks which need to be confronted alone', as individuals rather than working together with fellow citizens. 'The other side of individualisation seems to be the corrosion and slow disintegration of citizenship.'

# GLOBALISATION

Globalisation is the process by which societies become increasingly interconnected. As a result, events in one part of the world have a growing impact on events in other parts. Giddens (2009) states that globalisation involves 'the coming together of political, social, cultural and economic factors' across the world.

## MULTINATIONAL CORPORATIONS

Multinational corporations are companies that produce goods and/or provide services in more than one country – for example, Sony, BP, Apple, Ford, HSBC and Nestlé. Multinationals account for over two-thirds of global trade and their production, employment, marketing and financial decisions are based on global perspectives.

## GLOBAL FINANCE

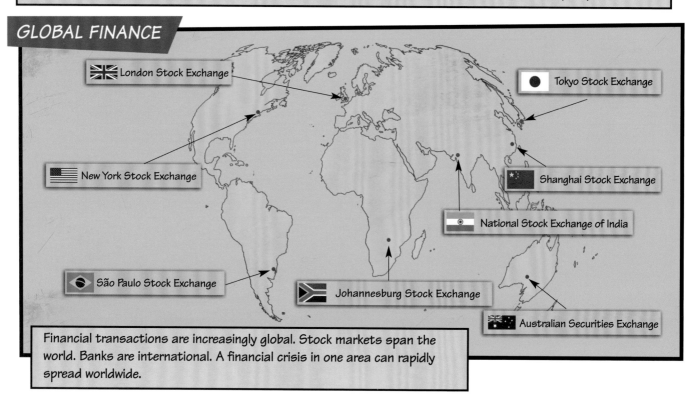

Financial transactions are increasingly global. Stock markets span the world. Banks are international. A financial crisis in one area can rapidly spread worldwide.

## POLITICAL GLOBALISATION

The United Nations aims to promote peace, better living standards and human rights (193 member states).

The World Bank offers loans and advice and aims for a world free from poverty (188 members).

The European Union is an economic and political partnership (28 member countries).

The IMF, an agency of the UN, provides member countries with financial advice and assistance (188 members).

The African Union encourages cooperation between African nations (54 members).

The Arab League aims to draw its members closer together and represent their interests (22 members).

More and more countries are becoming members of worldwide and regional organisations.

## CULTURAL GLOBALISATION

Music, films, fashion have a growing worldwide audience.

## CULTURAL IMPERIALISM

I BRING YOU DISNEY, MTV, NIKE, STARBUCKS, KFC, APPLE, GOOGLE...

Some researchers see globalisation as *cultural imperialism* – the West imposing its culture on the rest of the world and sweeping away local cultures.

## GLOCALISATION

WE DO IT OUR WAY.

Some researchers see a process of *glocalisation* – a mixing of cultures in which the global and local meet and create something new, for example, Bollywood musicals, Chinese tacos and Japanese rap.

## GLOBAL RISK SOCIETY

Ulrich Beck argues that many of the risks today are global and can only be dealt with by global organisations. These risks include pollution, global warming and over-fishing.

## DETRADITIONALISATION

Demonstrating for democracy in Tahrir Square, Egypt, in 2011 after 30 years of dictatorship. Giddens argues that globalisation challenges established ways and traditions by presenting alternative views. This can lead to *detraditionalisation*.

# THE NETWORK SOCIETY

Born in Spain, Professor Manuel Castells has taught in universities across the world. He believes we now live in a new type of society – *the network society*. There have always been social networks. The difference today is that these networks have been transformed by information technology and the Internet. 'Digital networks are global as they know no boundaries. Thus the network society is a global society' (Castells, 2004).

## THE GLOBAL ECONOMY

'The new economy is organised around global networks of capital, management and information. Access to technological know-how is at the roots of productivity and competitiveness.' These networks are 'enacted by light-speed-operating information technologies' (Castells, 2000).

Poppy growing for opium in Afghanistan.

Laundering drug money to make it appear to come from a legal source.

Those at the centre of global economic networks tend to grow richer, those excluded grow poorer. The gap between them is widening. The poor are increasingly drawn into global crime networks – e.g. drug networks which include poppy and coca growers, traffickers, street gangs, money launderers and drug barons.

## SOCIAL MOVEMENTS

In *Networks of Outrage and Hope: Social Movements in an Internet Age* (2012), Manuel Castells argues that the Internet and wireless communication played a crucial part in recent social movements. They have helped to create and organise networks of protest, they have challenged the powerful and 'turned fear into outrage and outrage into hope for a better humanity'.

## THE TUNISIAN REVOLUTION

In December 2010, in a small town in Tunisia, Mohamed Bouazizi set himself on fire in protest against police corruption. The demonstration which followed in support of him was filmed and placed on the Internet. The Tunisian revolution which overthrew the dictatorship had begun. Twitter, Facebook, YouTube and mobile phones were widely used to record, publicise and organise demonstrations and debates.

## OCCUPY WALL STREET

In 2011, 20,000 people occupied Wall Street, the financial district of New York, protesting against corporate greed and malpractice. Hundreds of thousands had lost their homes and the financial system was on the verge of collapse. Outrage swept the USA. 'Born on the Internet', a new social network developed. Protest camps spread across the USA, most with their own website. Facebook, Twitter and mobile phones were used to mobilise, organise, photograph and video.

# THE REINVENTION SOCIETY

In *Reinvention* (2013), Professor Anthony Elliott presents a picture of the reinvention society. He sees the reinvention of persons, bodies, careers, corporations, networks and places as a wide-ranging and fast-growing global trend. He argues that this process is largely directed by globalisation – by the demands of a global economy for constant innovation and change. In Elliott's words, 'globalisation spells endless reinvention'.

## THE REINVENTION OF PERSONS AND BODIES

The global economy demands 'flexibility, adaptability and transformation'. These demands reach down to the individual level – to self-concepts and relationships. The result is 'the reconstruction and reinvention of self'.

## THE REINVENTION OF CAREERS

People are increasingly hired for projects on short-term contracts. As a result, they must be flexible and reinvent themselves – learn new skills, be ready to 'embrace change' and keep pace with a rapidly changing job market.

## THE REINVENTION OF CORPORATIONS

The global economy is increasingly competitive, changeable and turbulent. This requires corporations to constantly reinvent – 'redesign, rebrand, refinance' and restructure their business practices.

## THE REINVENTION OF PLACES

According to Elliott, today's reinvention reflects 'a culture obsessed with having the biggest, best, largest, shiniest and newest of everything'. The prime example is Dubai, with its 'monumental architecture, mega-shopping malls for excessive consumption, lavish hotels, and blockbuster sports and entertainment events'.

# COMMON SENSE

*The American Soldier* (Stouffer,1949), a large scale study of US soldiers during World War II, was criticised as stating the obvious. In a review, Paul Lazarsfeld (1949) invented some findings which, at the time, appeared obvious and based on common sense. But they were 'the direct opposite of what was actually found'. This shows the importance of research and the problems of common sense.

Common sense: Soldiers from the hot southern states of the USA were better able to cope with the heat of the South Pacific than those from the northern states. Wrong: No difference.

Common sense: Soldiers were more eager to go home during the fighting than after the war ended. Wrong: More eager after the war ended.

Common sense: Better educated soldiers had more psychological problems than those with less education. Wrong: The less educated had more problems.

Common sense (in 1949): White soldiers were more eager for promotion than black soldiers. Wrong: Black soldiers were more eager.

# REFERENCES

Atkinson, J.M. (1978). *Discovering Suicide*. London: Macmillan.

Ball, S.J. (2003). *Class Strategies and the Education Market: The Middle Classes and Social Advantage*. London: RoutledgeFalmer.

Baudrillard, J. (1994). *Simulation and Simulacra*. Ann Arbor, MI: University of Michigan Press.

Bauman, Z. (2003). *Liquid Love*. Cambridge: Polity Press.

Bauman, Z. (2012). *Liquid Modernity* (2nd edition). Cambridge: Polity Press.

Beck, U. (1992). *Risk Society: Towards a New Modernity*. London: Sage.

Beck, U. & Beck-Gernsheim, E. (2001). *Individualisation*. London: Sage.

Becker, H.S. (1963). *Outsiders*. New York: The Free Press.

Becker, H.S. (1970). *Sociological Work*. New Brunswick: Transaction Books.

Bourdieu, P. (1984). *Distinction: A Social Critique of the Judgement of Taste*. London: Routledge & Kegan Paul.

Brazier, C. (1995). African Village. *New Internationalist*, June.

Castells, M. (2000). *The End of the Millennium: The Information Age*. Cambridge, MA: Blackwell.

Castells, M. (2004). *The Rise of the Network Society* (2nd edition). Oxford: Blackwell.

Castells, M. (2012). *Networks of Outrage and Hope: Social Movements in the Internet Age*. Cambridge: Polity Press.

Collins, P.H. (1990). *Black Feminist Thought: Knowledge, Consciousness, and the Politics of Empowerment*. New York: Routledge.

Durkheim, E. (1964). *The Rules of Sociological Method*. New York: The Free Press.

Durkheim, E. (1968). *The Elementary Forms of the Religious Life*. London: Allen & Unwin.

Durkheim, E. (1970). *Suicide: A Study in Sociology*. London: Routledge & Kegan Paul.

Elliott, A. (2013). *Reinvention*. Abingdon: Routledge.

Foucault, M. (2009). *History of Madness*. Abingdon: Routledge.

Garfinkel, H. (1967). *Studies in Ethnomethodology*. Englewood Cliffs, NJ: Prentice-Hall.

Giddens, A. (1991). *Modernity and Self-Identity: Self and Society in the Late Modern Age*. Cambridge: Polity Press.

Giddens, A. (1999). *Runaway World: How Globalisation is Reshaping Our Lives*. London: Profile Books.

Giddens, A. (2009). *Sociology* (6th edition). Cambridge: Polity Press.

Goffman, E. (1959). *The Presentation of Self in Everyday Life*. Harmondsworth: Penguin.

Hall, E.T. (1973). *The Silent Language*. New York: Doubleday.

Lazarsfeld, P.F. (1949). The American Soldier: An Expository Review. *Public Opinion Quarterly, 13*, 377-404.

Malinowski, B. (1954). *Magic, Science and Religion and Other Essays*. New York: Anchor Books.

Marx, K. & Engels, F. (2008). *The Communist Manifesto*. Oxford: Oxford University Press.

Mead, G.H. (1934). *Mind, Self and Society*. University of Chicago Press: Chicago.

Morris, T.P. (1957). *The Criminal Area: A Study in Social Ecology*. London: Routledge & Kegan Paul.

Murdock, G.P. (1949). *Social Structure*. New York: Macmillan.

Reay, D. (1998). *Class Work: Mothers' Involvement in their Children's Primary Schooling*. London: UCL Press.

Reay, D., David, M.E., & Ball, S. (2005). *Degrees of Choice: Class, Race, Gender and Higher Education*. Stoke on Trent: Trentham Books.

Schapera, I. (1971). *Married Life in African Tribes*. Harmondsworth: Penguin.

Shaw, C.R. & McKay, H.D. (1942). *Juvenile Delinquency and Urban Areas*. Chicago: University of Chicago Press.

Weber, M. (1949). *The Methodology of the Social Sciences*. New York: The Free Press.

Weber, M. (1958). *The Protestant Ethic and the Spirit of Capitalism*. New York: The Free Press.

Weber, M. (1964). *The Theory of Social and Economic Organisations*. New York: The Free Press.

Williams, W.L. (1986). *The Spirit and the Flesh: Sexual Diversity in American Indian Culture*. Boston: Beacon Press.

Wilson, J.W. (1996). *When Work Disappears: The World of the New Urban Poor*. New York: Random House.